I Love You No Matter
A Celebration of Parents' Unconditional Love

Kurosh Taromi

Title: I Love You No Matter
        A Celebration of Parents' Unconditional Love
Author: Kurosh Taromi
Illustrator: Kurosh Taromi (Using Midjourney)

© 2024 Golden Maple Publications
ISBN: 978-1-0690106-0-5
www.golden-maple.com
kuroshtaromi@gmail.com

Dedication

To my beloved parents, Yadollah and Farah,
Though you are no longer with me,
The gift of your unconditional love lives on—
A guiding light that will keep me strong for as long as I exist.
This book is a tribute to the love you gave so freely,
And a reminder of your beautiful words that resonate in my heart.

K.T.

I love you no matter if the sky is gray,
Or if it smiles on a sunshiny day.

And if we're soaked in nasty weather,
I don't mind it as long as we are together.

I love you no matter if you're short or tall,
If you have big ears or no ears at all.

In every moment, as time goes by,
I admire you whether you're brave or shy.

I love you no matter if you lose or win,
If you are overweight or you are very thin.

In whatever game and every quest,
To me, you're always the very best.

I love you no matter if you're feeling blue,
When tears come down and troubles brew.

When lights are far and shadows are near,
I'll hold you tight, I'm always here.

I love you no matter if you dodge bedtime,
When monsters hide and ogres climb.

Together we'll laugh and chase them away,
With giggles and hugs till night turns to day.

I love you no matter if you dream or wake,
In every step in every path you take.

Your daring dreams are stars in the night,
I'll help you find your guiding light.

I love you no matter if you're quiet or loud,
Whether you sigh or shout so proud.

In whisper or cheer, in every song,
With you, my dear, I'll sing along.

I love you no matter if the world spins fast,
Or if moments forever seem to last.

In every laugh and every sigh,
My love for you will never die.

I love you no matter if you get things right,
Or if you stumble with all your might.

In every effort, big or small,
I'll catch you always if you fall.

I love you no matter if you're feeling wild,
With giggles and games, my playful child.

In every fun and joyful spree,
I'll love you through your wiggly glee.

I love you no matter if you wander free,
Or if you need to sit with me.

In every smile, in every frown,
My love will never let you down.

I love you no matter if life gets tough,
When things go wrong or feel too rough.

In stormy times, when a hug is due,
My love will always comfort you.

I love you no matter if you're near or far,
Or if you become a travelling star.

In every place you choose to roam,
My love will guide you back to home.

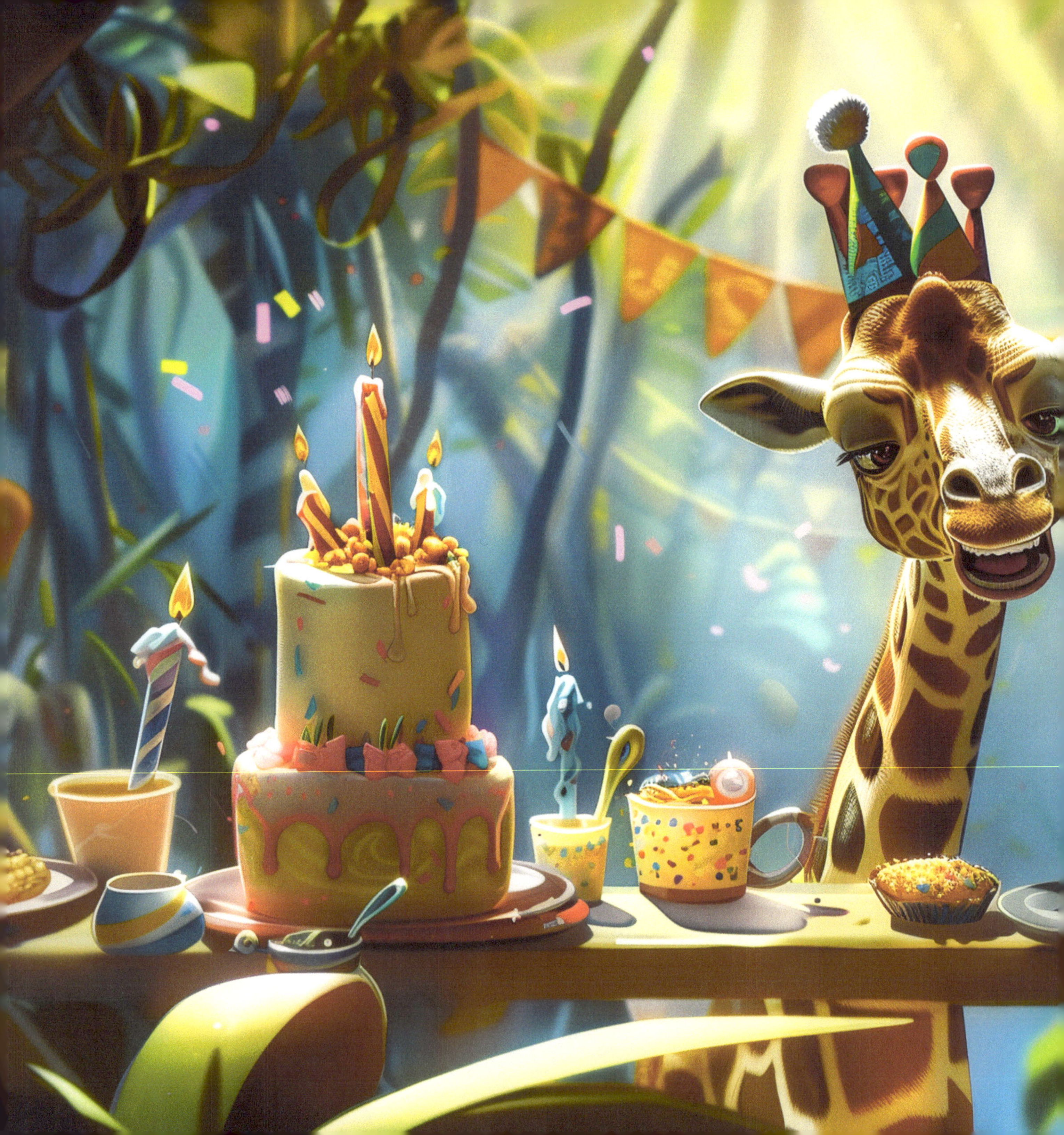

I love you no matter if it's easy or tense,
If love is wise or doesn't make any sense.

Why is it like this? I have no clue,
I want to celebrate every day with you.

www.ingramcontent.com/pod-product-compliance
Lightning Source LLC
LaVergne TN
LVHW072059070426
835508LV00002B/179